SPINOSAURUS

The Child's World®
childsworld.com

Published by The Child's World®
1980 Lookout Drive • Mankato, MN 56003-1705
800-599-READ • www.childsworld.com

Acknowledgments
The Child's World®: Mary Berendes, Publishing Director
The Design Lab: Design
Heidi Schoof: Photo Research
Michael Miller and Sarah Miller: Editing

Content Adviser
Peter Makovicky, PhD, Curator • Field Museum, Chicago, Illinois

Original Cover Art
Todd S. Marshall

Photo Credits
© Christian Darkin/Science Source: 17; Christian Jegou/Science Source: 20; De
Agostini Picture Library/Getty Images: 7, 16, 18, 19; Francois Gohier/Science
Source: 21; Franck Robichon/epa/Corbis: 12; Jayson Kowinsky/www.fossilguy.
com: 10, 15; Joe Tucciarone/Science Source: 9; Jonathan Blair/Corbis: 23, 25;
Ric Ergenbright/Corbis: 26; slobo/iStockphoto.com: design element (paper);
Todd S. Marshall: 1, 5, 6; Universal History Archive/Contributor/Getty Images:
11; Yann Arthus-Bertrand/Corbis: 8

ISBN 9781631439827
LCCN 2014959653

Printed in the United States of America
Mankato, MN
July, 2015
PA02263

CONTENTS

CHAPTER ONE
Going Fishing

A *Spinosaurus* (spy-no-SAWR-uhss) stood absolutely still at the lake's edge. The water came up to his knees and lapped gently against his leathery skin. The dinosaur's long, narrow head was lowered. His eyes, unblinking, stared into the water. He did not move a muscle.

Two enormous dragonflies swooped overhead, one right behind the other. Their huge wings made a loud whirring sound. But the noise did not bother *Spinosaurus*. He stood as still as a rock.

The sun was behind the big dinosaur, and he cast a shadow on the lake. After a few minutes, a fish swam into the shaded area. It paused for a second and then zipped away. A moment later, another fish glided into the shade. Its silvery back caught the dinosaur's eye. The heart of the big **reptile** began to beat a little faster. Yet, he stood still like a statue.

Spinosaurus's terrifying claws, sharp teeth, and high level of intelligence made it a ferocious hunter.

The fish turned and began to slowly swim away. Suddenly, faster than a lightning bolt, *Spinosaurus* shot his head into the water. Then he lifted it into the air. The fish thrashed violently in the dinosaur's mouth, but *Spinosaurus* held on tight. He turned his head upward, opening his jaws. The fish disappeared down the dinosaur's throat. *Spinosaurus* stood quietly for a few seconds and then lowered his head. Again, his unblinking eyes peered into the water. He did not move a muscle.

Unlike many larger dinosaurs, Spinosaurus was able to move at swift speeds.

CHAPTER TWO

What Is a Spinosaurus?

A *Spinosaurus* was a dinosaur that lived from about 100 million to 93 million years ago. Its name is taken from the Latin word *spina*, which means "thorn" or "spine," and the Greek word *sauros*, which means "lizard." The name refers to a series of tall spines rising from the dinosaur's backbone.

Spinosaurus (shown here) was not the only dinosaur with an interesting back. Stegosaurus (steg-oh-SAWR-uhss) was a plant eater whose back had a row of pointed plates. Ankylosaurus (an-kuh-low-SAWR-uhss) had a back that was covered by armor-like plates.

Like a crocodile's head, Spinosaurus's head was quite narrow and was filled with many sharp teeth that were perfect for cutting.

Spinosaurus was gigantic. In fact, it may have been the longest meat-eating animal to ever walk the earth. An adult grew to be almost 50 feet (15 meters) in length. The dinosaur's spines added greatly to its height. When *Spinosaurus* stood upright, the top of its back measured about 18 feet (5.5 m) from the ground. The animal weighed as much as 5 tons (4.5 metric tons).

The reptile's skull was 5 to 6 feet (1.5 to 1.8 m) long. *Spinosaurus*'s head was narrow like that of a crocodile, and the dinosaur had powerful muscles that could snap the jaws shut in a flash. From front to back, the mouth was filled with straight, sharp teeth.

Spinosaurus moved on two huge legs. Its arms were much smaller but were powerful nonetheless. Fingers and toes ended in sharp claws that were perfect for tearing flesh.

Scientists believe *Spinosaurus* moved quickly on its two gigantic hind legs. It is possible to estimate *Spinosaurus*'s speed by comparing fossilized dinosaur tracks to the creature's weight and the length of its legs.

The creature had a strong, muscular neck and a heavy, thick tail. In addition to the dinosaur's great size and fearsome looks, it had one other outstanding feature. Running down its back, from the neck to the base of the tail, was a huge sail. The sail was held up by the row of spines that rose from the dinosaur's backbone. The

This huge Spinosaurus skeleton is at the National Geographic Museum in Washington, DC.

shortest spines were at the neck and tail. The tallest spines were in the middle of the sail, with some reaching a height of almost 6 feet (1.8 m). Each spine was broad and flat, like a sword. Skin covered the spines, forming a web between them.

CHAPTER THREE

Who Discovered Spinosaurus?

In 1912, Richard Markgraf discovered *Spinosaurus* bones. Markgraf worked for German **paleontologist** Ernst Stromer von Reichenbach. At the time, Stromer and his team of **fossil** hunters were working in Egypt, which is located in northern Africa. They were searching for the remains of **ancient** animals.

In the early 1900s, transporting fossils (such as this Diplodocus leg) was often costly, time-consuming, and potentially destructive.

This Spinosaurus model is a copy of the skeleton that Ernst Stromer discovered in 1915.

Over a period of several years, they were quite successful. They found the fossil remains of plants, turtles, crocodiles, fish, and dinosaurs. Among the dinosaur remains was a skeleton with tall, blade-like spines sticking up from the bones in its back. In 1915, Stromer wrote a paper describing this new dinosaur. He gave it the name *Spinosaurus*.

Stromer's team packed up his entire collection of fossils to send back to Germany. Stromer planned to return home and start working on them. He needed to clean the fossils, glue them back together, and figure out what kinds of animals they came from. Unfortunately, it took years for the fossils to arrive. But once they did, Stromer laid out the *Spinosaurus* bones as he believed they had been positioned in the living dinosaur. He wrote about the skeleton and took pictures of it. Everyone who saw the bones agreed that *Spinosaurus* was a most unusual dinosaur.

A Terrible Ending

Between 1911 and 1914, Ernst Stromer and his helpers worked hard in northern Africa. Some of his helpers were from Europe, and others were native Egyptians. Together, they lived and worked in an **oasis** in the western desert of Egypt. They found many fossils that were thought to be about 100 million years old. Once the fossil hunting ended, Stromer arranged for his finds to be shipped to Munich, Germany. Then he returned home.

Shortly afterward, World War I broke out. Shipping the fossils became the last thing on anyone's mind, and no one sent them to Germany. When the war ended, Stromer again arranged to have his fossils shipped.

Finally, in 1922, they arrived in Germany. Stromer excitedly began to unpack the fossils. But when he saw them after so many years, his heart sank. Many of the fossils had been packed poorly. Some had broken to pieces on their trip from Egypt.

Nonetheless, Stromer worked hard to put them back together. It was frustrating work. Some of the fossils fell apart when they were cleaned. Some had chunks missing that Stromer knew had been packed. He worked long hours piecing them together, and he kept everything in a museum for safekeeping.

In 1939, World War II broke out. With bombs going off everywhere, museum workers all over Germany hurried to protect their valuables. They stashed great works of art, precious jewels, rare fossils, and many other treasures in secret hiding places. Because he refused to join the Nazis—the political party that controlled Germany at that time—Stromer's request to have his **specimens** moved was denied. His collection

was left behind. During a bombing raid on Munich, the city's museum was demolished. Nothing was left of Stromer's fossils. His precious *Spinosaurus* skeleton had been turned to dust.

CHAPTER FOUR

Why Did *Spinosaurus* Have That Sail?

Perhaps the most unusual thing about *Spinosaurus* was its sail. Paleontologists have several ideas about the purpose of the structure. One idea has to do with body temperature.

If dinosaurs were cold-blooded animals, their body temperatures went up and down with

Spinosaurus undoubtedly had a unique appearance. But although it was the largest of its kind, it was not the only sail-backed dinosaur.

the outside temperatures. When it was cold outside, the reptiles' blood was cool, and the animals were not very active. When it was hot outside, the dinosaurs' blood warmed

Spinosaurus's sail might have helped control the dinosaur's body temperature. If cold-blooded animals lose too much body heat, they often go into a deep sleep called hibernation (hy-bur-NAY-shuhn).

up, and the reptiles became more active. Perhaps *Spinosaurus* stood in the warm sun with its sail skin spread out. The blood running through the sail would warm up quickly, helping the dinosaur's body to warm up as well. If the dinosaur got too hot, it could stand in the shade or turn its sail in another direction to cool off. This would cause the body temperature to fall.

Perhaps the sail on Spinosaurus's back helped scare off enemy dinosaurs. However, this may not have worked if the attacker were another Spinosaurus.

Some scientists think the sail was related to finding a mate. Perhaps *Spinosaurus* males showed off their handsome sails to females. The most attractive males would have had no trouble finding mates.

Others believe the sail was used for defense. Maybe *Spinosaurus* spread its mighty sail to scare off attackers. Enemies would see that big sail and think *Spinosaurus* was even more enormous than it really was. However, some scientists say this idea does not make any sense. They believe *Spinosaurus* was so huge that nothing would have wanted to attack it anyway.

In recent years, some scientists have put forth one other idea. They point out that the dinosaur's spines were not thin and delicate. Instead, they were quite broad and strong. Such strong spines could have supported a thick, heavy structure. Perhaps instead of a thin sail, *Spinosaurus* had a big hump on its back. The hump might have stored fat that could have helped the dinosaur survive if it were unable to find food. Because *Spinosaurus* lived in a harsh **environment**, it may have been tough to find food. Like so many other things about dinosaurs, the mystery of *Spinosaurus*'s sail might never be solved.

It is possible that Spinosaurus ate its own kind. But what if Spinosaurus were hungry and could not readily find a meal? Maybe the dinosaur had a fat-filled hump on its back that would have helped it survive if food were scarce.

Spinosaurus was not the only animal with spines rising from its backbone. Another large sail-backed dinosaur named *Ouranosaurus* (oo-ran-oh-SAWR-uhss) (below, right) also had them. *Ouranosaurus* lived at about the same time and in the same place where *Spinosaurus* lived. However, *Ouranosaurus* ate plants and was only about 24 feet (7.3 m) in length. The spines that stuck up from its backbone were flat like those of *Spinosaurus*.

Dimetrodon (dy-MET-ruh-don) was another sail-backed animal. This reptile lived about 50 million years before dinosaurs appeared on

Earth. *Dimetrodon* weighed more than 500 pounds (227 kilograms). It walked on four short legs, with its body close to the ground. Its sail was quite impressive, rising high above the animal's back. Its spines were slender, not broad and flat.

Some modern animals also have long spines rising from their backbones. The buffalo is a large, shaggy animal that lives on the plains of North America. Right behind its neck is a huge hump. Spines from the buffalo's backbone support the hump. The spines are broad and flat, much like those of *Ouranosaurus* and *Spinosaurus*.

CHAPTER FIVE

What Did Spinosaurus Eat?

To figure out what dinosaurs ate, scientists look at the animals' teeth and bodies. Meat-eating dinosaurs were built for tracking down **prey**. Many had strong back legs and were good runners. Meat eaters also had sharp teeth for tearing flesh. Often, their teeth were **notched** and curved backward. Plant-eating dinosaurs were usually slower, bulkier animals. They often had many dull teeth that were good for grinding down plant material.

It appears that *Spinosaurus* ate fish. Its head was long, low, and narrow—much like the head of a crocodile. A head with a narrow snout would have sliced easily through water. The dinosaur's teeth were long, straight, and pointed. They would have been excellent for grabbing and holding a struggling fish.

Spinosaurus might also have hunted land animals. And it may have dined on animals that had already died. A dinosaur cousin of *Spinosaurus* was found with fish scales within its rib cage. This shows that some relatives of *Spinosaurus* ate fish. Perhaps one day, scientists will discover a *Spinosaurus* skeleton complete with its last meal. Then we will have a better idea about what the dinosaur ate.

Spinosaurus probably would have enjoyed feasting on this prehistoric fish!

CHAPTER SIX

Still Looking for Spinosaurus

Some paleontologists today are still looking for *Spinosaurus* remains. They are making trips to northern Africa, where the reptile was first found. They hope to learn more about this unusual dinosaur and its life. However, the work is slow and difficult. It is not easy to plan a fossil-hunting trip. The first problem usually is figuring out how to pay for the trip. The scientists need money to pay for travel, equipment, food, and helpers.

Before they set out, paleontologists try to learn everything about the places where they will be hunting. Will they be close to town? Where can they buy food? Where can they hire some

Paleontologists uncovered this fossilized Dinogorgon skull in Africa. Dinogorgon was a prehistoric creature that roamed Africa before dinosaurs even walked the earth. By studying the shape of its teeth, paleontologists know that Dinogorgon was a meat eater.

help? What is the weather like? Will they get around by driving or by hiking? Do they need to take any special clothes, supplies, or medicine? What kinds of maps will they need? What if they make a great discovery and need more time and money to

Paleontologists continue to search Africa for additional Spinosaurus fossils. Their work is challenging, but it will ultimately help us learn more about this mysterious sail-backed dinosaur and the world in which it lived.

check it out? Sometimes it is also a problem to get permission to hunt dinosaurs. Not every country will allow people to come in and look for fossils. So before paleontologists arrive, they need to discuss certain things. What if the scientists discover a new dinosaur? Can they go ahead and dig it up? Who gets to keep the skeleton? Can the scientists take the bones out of the country if they promise to send them back? Many things must be decided.

In the last few years, many paleontologists have faced these problems. Nonetheless, some have continued to search northern Africa. They have discovered some *Spinosaurus* teeth and a few bones. But a complete skeleton has not yet been found. There is still plenty of work to do.

GLOSSARY

ancient (AYN-shunt) Something that is ancient is very old. Paleontologists study ancient life.

environment (en-VYE-ruhn-muhnt) An environment is made up of the things that surround a living creature, such as the air and soil. *Spinosaurus* lived in a harsh environment.

fossil (FOSS-uhl) A fossil is something left behind by an ancient plant or animal. Ernst Stromer and his team searched for fossils in Egypt.

notched (NOCHT) Something that is notched has a V-shaped cut or groove in it. Meat-eating dinosaurs often had notched teeth.

oasis (oh-AY-siss) An oasis is an area with plants and water within a desert. Stromer and his team worked in an oasis in a desert in western Egypt.

paleontologist (pale-ee-uhn-TOL-uh-jist) A paleontologist is a person who studies ancient living things. Paleontologists discovered the remains of a *Spinosaurus* in the early 1900s.

prey (PRAY) Prey are animals that are hunted and eaten by other animals. *Spinosaurus* hunted prey such as fish.

reptile (REP-tile) A reptile is an animal that breathes air, has a backbone, and is usually covered with scales or plates. *Spinosaurus* was a reptile.

specimens (SPESS-uh-muhnz) Specimens are things used to represent an entire group. It took a great deal of time for Stromer's dinosaur specimens to reach Germany.

TRIASSIC PERIOD

Date: 248 million to 208 million years ago

Fossils: *Coelophysis, Cynodont, Desmatosuchus, Eoraptor, Gerrothorax, Peteinoaurus, Placerias, Plateosaurus, Postosuchus, Procompsognathus, Riojasaurus, Saltopus, Teratosaurus, Thecodontosaurus*

Distinguishing Features: For the most part, the climate in the Triassic period was hot and dry. The first true mammals appeared during this period, as well as turtles, frogs, salamanders, and lizards. Corals could also be found in oceans at this time, although large reefs such as the ones we have today did not yet exist. Evergreen trees made up much of the plant life.

JURASSIC PERIOD

Date: 208 million to 144 million years ago

Fossils: *Allosaurus, Apatosaurus, Brachiosaurus, Compsognathus, Dilophosaurus, Diplodocus, Hybodus, Kentrosaurus, Megalosaurus, Saurolophus, Segisaurus, Seismosaurus, Stegosaurus, Supersaurus, Ultrasaurus, Vulcanodon*

Distinguishing Features: The climate of the Jurassic period was warm and moist. The first birds appeared during this period. Plant life was also greener and more widespread. Sharks began swimming in Earth's oceans. Although dinosaurs did not even exist at the beginning of the Triassic period, they ruled Earth by Jurassic times. A minor mass extinction occurred toward the end of the Jurassic period.

THE GEOLOGIC TIME SCALE

CRETACEOUS PERIOD

Date: 144 million to 65 million years ago

Fossils: *Alamosaurus, Albertosaurus, Ankylosaurus, Argentinosaurus, Bagaceratops, Baryonyx, Carnotaurus, Centrosaurus, Corythosaurus, Didelphodon, Edmontonia, Edmontosaurus, Gallimimus, Gigantosaurus, Hadrosaurus, Hypsilophodon, Iguanodon, Kronosaurus, Lambeosaurus, Maiasaura, Megaraptor, Nodosaurus, Oviraptor, Parasaurolophus, Protoceratops, Psittacosaurus, Saltasaurus, Sarcosuchus, Saurolophus, Sauropelta, Saurornithoides, Segnosaurus, Spinosaurus, Stygimoloch, Styracosaurus, Tarbosaurus, Thescelosaurus, Torosaurus, Trachodon, Triceratops, Troodon, Tyrannosaurus rex, Utahraptor, Velociraptor*

Distinguishing Features: The climate of the Cretaceous period was fairly mild. Flowering plants first appeared in this period, and many modern plants developed. With flowering plants came a greater diversity of insect life. Birds further developed into two types: flying and flightless. A wider variety of mammals also existed. At the end of this period came a great mass extinction that wiped out the dinosaurs, along with several other groups of animals.

DID YOU KNOW?

- *Spinosaurus* had a somewhat flexible back. This means that the dinosaur might have arched its back to fully spread the sail.

- Although other dinosaurs were sail-backed, *Spinosaurus* had the tallest sail.

- Some paleontologists believe *Spinosaurus* was a peaceful reptile that did not fight with or attack other dinosaurs. They believe this because *Spinosaurus* could not risk tearing its sail during a fight.

HOW TO LEARN MORE

At the Library

Bailey, Gerry. *Spinosaurus*. New York, NY: Crabtree, 2011.

West, David. *Spinosaurus and Other Dinosaurs and Reptiles from the Upper Cretaceous*. New York, NY: Gareth Stevens, 2012.

On the Web

Visit our Web site for links about *Spinosaurus*: **childsworld.com/links**

Note to Parents, Teachers, and Librarians: We routinely verify our Web links to make sure they are safe and active sites. So encourage your readers to check them out!

American Museum of Natural History: *To view numerous dinosaur fossils, as well as the fossils of several ancient mammals*
Address: Central Park West at 79th Street, New York, NY 10024
Phone: (212) 769-5100

Carnegie Museum of Natural History: *To view a variety of dinosaur skeletons, as well as fossils related to other reptiles, amphibians, and fish that are now extinct*
Address: 4400 Forbes Avenue, Pittsburgh, PA 15213
Phone: (412) 622-3131

Dinosaur National Monument: *To view a huge deposit of dinosaur bones in a natural setting*
Address: 4545 East Highway 40, Dinosaur, CO 81610
Phone: (970) 374-3000
 –OR–
Dinosaur National Monument (Quarry):
Address: 11625 East 1500 South, Jensen, UT 84035
Phone: (435) 781-7700

Museum of the Rockies: *To see real dinosaur fossils, as well as robotic replicas*
Address: Montana State University, 600 West Kagy Boulevard, Bozeman, MT 59717
Phone: (406) 994-2251 or (406) 994-DINO

National Museum of Natural History (Smithsonian Institution): *To see several dinosaur exhibits and take special behind-the-scenes tours*
Address: 10th Street and Constitution Avenue, N.W., Washington, DC 20560
Phone: (202) 357-2700

INDEX

ABOUT THE AUTHOR

Susan H. Gray has bachelor's and master's degrees in zoology and has taught college-level courses in biology. She first fell in love with fossil hunting while studying paleontology in college. In her 25 years as an author, she has written many articles for scientists and researchers, and many science books for children. Susan enjoys gardening, traveling, and playing the piano. She and her husband, Michael, live in Cabot, Arkansas.